My World Your World

Christianity
This Is Our Faith

by Ruth Owen

With thanks to
Elizabeth Harewood
Association of Christian Teachers

Ruby Tuesday Books

Published in 2026 by Ruby Tuesday Books Ltd.
Copyright © 2026 Ruby Tuesday Books Ltd.

Editor: Mark J. Sachner
Design & Production: Tammy West

Photo Credits:

Alamy: Cover & 4B (Ray Evans), 11 (David Humphreys), 14T (Tim Moore), 16 (Ira Berger), 17B (Peek Creative Collective), 19T (Sipa US), 21L (Bjarki Reyr), 23 (Peter Treanor); iStock: 13B (Carmen K Sisson); Shutterstock: 1 (Sync Design Solutions), 2–3 Paul Shuang, 4T (Sew Cream Studio), 5 (By Drone Videos), 6T (Svetlana Vorotniak), 6L, 6R, 7L (Jorisvo), 7R (A-photography), 8T (wavebreakmedia), 8B (Cecil Bo Dzwowa), 9 (HASPhotos), 10T (antoinee), 10B (trabantos), 12 (Bill Perry), 13T (Cezary Wojtkowski/hramikona), 14B (Magdalena Kucova), 15 (WorldStockStudio), 17T (Jeanie333), 18, 19BL (Natasha Zakharova), 19BR (iuliia_n), 20 (Kzenon), 21R (Chekunov Aleksandr), 22 (antonina jurii mazokha/New Africa), 24 (Neirfy).

British Library Cataloguing in Publication Data (CIP) is available for this title.

ISBN 978-1-78856-209-6

Printed in Malta by Gutenberg Press

FSC
www.fsc.org

MIX
Paper | Supporting responsible forestry
FSC® C022612

www.rubytuesdaybooks.com

Contents

This Is Our Faith 4

Jesus, the Son 6

Living a Christian Life 8

Welcome to a Church! 10

Different Christian Families 12

How We Worship 14

Let's Celebrate! Christmas 16

Let's Celebrate! Easter 18

Welcome to a Baptism 20

Welcome to a Christian Wedding 22

Glossary and Index 24

Words shown in bold in the text are explained in the glossary.

This Is Our Faith

Christianity is a faith that began nearly 2000 years ago.

People who follow this faith are called Christians.

A Christian family praying together

Children in Thailand act out the birth of Jesus

Christians believe in one God who made the world and everything in it.

They believe that God sent his son Jesus Christ to be the **saviour** of the world.

"Christians believe that there is one God that exists as Father, Son and Holy Spirit. This is called the Holy Trinity.

"God is the Father."

"Jesus is the Son who came to Earth to save us from sin."

"The Holy Spirit is always with Christians, comforting us and helping us to obey God."

This is the huge "Christ the Redeemer" statue in Brazil. The word Christ means "God's chosen one".

Christianity began in the part of the world that we now call the Middle East. Over time, it spread all around the world.

Jesus, the Son

Christians believe that God's son Jesus was born as a baby to a Jewish family.

He lived with his mother Mary and his earthly father, Joseph, in Nazareth.

Jesus learned to be a carpenter like Joseph.

As an adult, Jesus taught people to love God, love others, forgive and be kind.

However, some people did not agree with Jesus' teachings.

A stained glass church window showing Jesus on the cross

The Roman leaders who ruled the land where Jesus lived had him put to death on a cross.

Christians believe that three days after Jesus died, he came back to life and returned to **heaven**.

The **symbol** of a cross is very important to Christians.

" Christians believe that God is perfect and holy, but sin separates people from him. "

" Jesus died on the cross to take the punishment for sin, so we can be close to God again. If we put our trust in Jesus, we can be friends with God. "

Living a Christian Life

Christians can pray to God anywhere.

Many Christians read from the **Bible** every day.

This family are saying grace, a special prayer to thank God for their meal.

Students in Zimbabwe reading the Bible in school

The Bible is a holy book that teaches Christians about God. It contains prayers, **psalms**, stories about the life of Jesus and wise teachings to help people live a Christian life.

The Bible says that Jesus helped people who were in need.

Christians try to do this, too. They might become **volunteers** at a **food bank** or help people who are homeless.

A food bank set up by a Christian group

Volunteer

Jesus taught us to "love thy neighbour". This means we should be kind and caring to all other people.

Welcome to a Church!

Many Christians go to a **church** to worship God.

A church can be a tiny, simple wooden building.

It may also be a huge cathedral with room to welcome more than 2000 worshippers.

A small, wooden church on Réunion Island in the Indian Ocean

The Metropolitan Cathedral in Liverpool, UK

Most churches have an aisle that leads to a special wooden or stone table called the **altar**.

This church in England is built from stone.

The altar table has a cross.

An organ for playing music

Benches, called pews, where the worshippers sit

Cushions for kneeling when praying

Aisle

Christian churches are often open all day so that people can visit and quietly pray on their own.

11

Different Christian Families

There are three main groups, or families, of Christianity – Protestant, Roman Catholic and Orthodox Christianity.

These three Christian families may worship in different ways.

But they all believe in God and Jesus, and they all read the Bible.

Some churches are very simple inside, while others have lots of candles, statues and pictures.

Within the three main Christian families there are thousands of different groups or **denominations**.

A statue of Mary and Jesus inside a Roman Catholic Church in Italy

Inside an Orthodox church in Latvia

Orthodox Christians may stand quietly and pray before special religious pictures called icons.

Inside a small, simple Methodist church in the United States

An icon might show Mary, Jesus or a **saint**.

Methodism is a denomination of Protestant Christianity.

How We Worship

Most churches have their main **service** on a Sunday morning.

A **vicar**, or priest, reads from the Bible and gives a talk called a **sermon**.

Everyone says prayers and sings hymns, which are songs that praise God.

Vicar

Wine

Wafer-like pieces of bread

During some church services, many Christians receive Holy Communion.

The vicar or priest **blesses** bread and wine on the altar.

Then, the worshippers receive a tiny piece of bread and a sip of wine, or sometimes grape juice.

These Orthodox Christian children are receiving Holy Communion for the first time.

Shared cup of juice

Priest

Holy Communion remembers the Last Supper when Jesus shared bread and wine with his followers, who were called **disciples**.

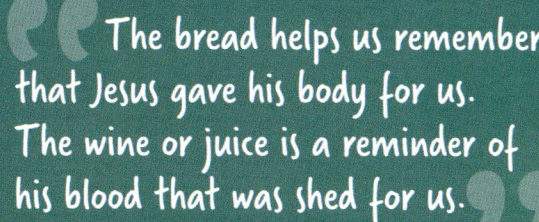

The bread helps us remember that Jesus gave his body for us. The wine or juice is a reminder of his blood that was shed for us.

Let's Celebrate! Christmas

Christmas is a joyful Christian festival that celebrates the birth of Jesus.

Most Christians celebrate Jesus' birthday on 25th December – Christmas Day.

Orthodox Christians celebrate on 7th January.

Joseph

Mary

Ecuadorian Americans in the United States take part in a Christmas parade.

" Mary and Joseph travelled to Bethlehem. There was no room for them at an inn, so they rested in a stable. It was there that Jesus was born. "

" Shepherds came to see the Son of God. Wise men from the East, following a star, also came to visit Jesus. "

The story of Jesus' birth is called the **Nativity**. People act out the story and decorate their homes and churches with Nativity scenes.

Angel

Shepherds

Wise men

Mary

Jesus

Joseph

A knitted Nativity scene

Cuzco Cathedral

At Christmas, people around the world celebrate by going to church, giving gifts and enjoying special meals.

Quechua people in Peru perform the Huaylia song and dance to celebrate Christmas Day.

Let's Celebrate! Easter

In spring, Christians celebrate Easter – their most important festival.

At this time, they remember how Jesus died and then came back to life. This joyful and hopeful event is called the Resurrection.

> "Jesus spent time with his followers. He told them to share the good news of God's forgiveness with people everywhere and to teach people how to love God. Then Jesus went up to heaven to be with his Father."

Jesus' followers visited his tomb and found it empty.

Jesus' disciples continued to share his teachings, and Christianity became a new faith.

An Easter parade in South Korea

Christians celebrate Easter by going to church services and gathering with friends and family.

Eggs are a symbol of new life. Some people paint eggs and eat chocolate eggs at Easter.

Some people celebrate by eating spicy hot cross buns.

"The Easter story shows us that God's love is stronger than anything – even death. We know that new life and hope are always possible."

Welcome to a Baptism

Christian families welcome a new baby to their faith at a baptism, or christening.

> " Godparents are friends or relatives of the baby's parents. They promise to help the baby learn about God and live a Christian life. "

Godmother

Father

Mother

Godfather

Godmother

The baby usually wears a long, white christening gown.

During a church service, the vicar or priest reads from the Bible. The baby's parents and godparents make special promises.

Water that has been blessed by the vicar or priest is placed in a special bowl called a font.

A small amount of water is poured over the baby's head.

At an Orthodox Christian baptism, the baby is gently dipped into the water three times as a sign of the Holy Trinity.

A Roman Catholic baptism in the Philippines

Font

Priest

An Orthodox Christian baptism in Russia

The water is a sign of a new beginning and becoming part of God's family.

Welcome to a Christian Wedding

Christian weddings usually take place in a church.

The bride and groom stand before a vicar or priest at the church's altar.

The couple make special promises, called vows, in front of God and their family.

During the wedding service there are hymns, prayers and readings from the Bible.

Wedding ring

The couple give each other wedding rings. A ring has no beginning or end. It is a symbol that the couple's love and promises will go on forever.

After the church service, everyone goes to a party, called a wedding reception, to celebrate with eating and dancing!

A couple make their vows at a Christian wedding in China.

"The bride and groom promise that they will stay together for better, for worse, for richer, for poorer, in sickness and in health until death parts them."

GLOSSARY

altar
In a church, a special table at the front where a vicar or priest leads prayers and Holy Communion.

Bible
A holy book. The Christian Bible has two main parts. The first part is also sacred to Jews. Christians call it the Old Testament. The second part, called the New Testament, tells the story of Jesus and how Christianity began.

bless
To ask for God's love and protection.

church
A building where Christians worship.

denomination
A branch of Christianity. Different denominations share the same beliefs but may worship in different ways.

disciple
In Christianity, a person who follows Jesus and learns from his teachings. Jesus had 12 main disciples.

food bank
A special place in a community where people who do not have enough to eat can go to get free food.

heaven
In Christian beliefs, a joyful, perfect place where God lives.

Nativity
The story of Jesus' birth. It comes from the word "nativitas", which means "birth".

psalm
A song, poem or prayer that a person sings or says when worshipping God.

saint
A person that Christians remember for helping others and having a strong faith. For example, Saint Francis of Assisi is remembered for caring for animals.

saviour
A person who saves others.

sermon
A special talk given by a religious leader that teaches about God and how to live a good life.

service
A gathering to pray, sing and learn about God.

sin
In Christian beliefs, the things people do or don't do that displease God.

symbol
Something that stands for something else – for example, a heart shape is a symbol for love.

vicar
A Christian religious leader, also called a priest, minister or pastor.

volunteer
A person who gives their time for free to help others.

INDEX

B
baptisms 20–21
Bible (the) 8–9, 12, 14, 20, 22

C
Christmas 16–17
churches 7, 10–11, 12–13, 14, 17, 19, 20, 22–23
crosses 7, 11

D
denominations of Christianity 12–13

E
Easter 18–19

H
Holy Communion 14–15
Holy Spirit (the) 5
Holy Trinity (the) 5, 21

I
icons 13

J
Jesus Christ 4–5, 6–7, 8–9, 12–13, 15, 16–17, 18
Joseph 6, 16–17

M
Mary 6, 12–13, 16–17

N
Nativity (the) 4, 16–17

V
vicars and priests 14–15, 20–21, 22

W
weddings 22–23

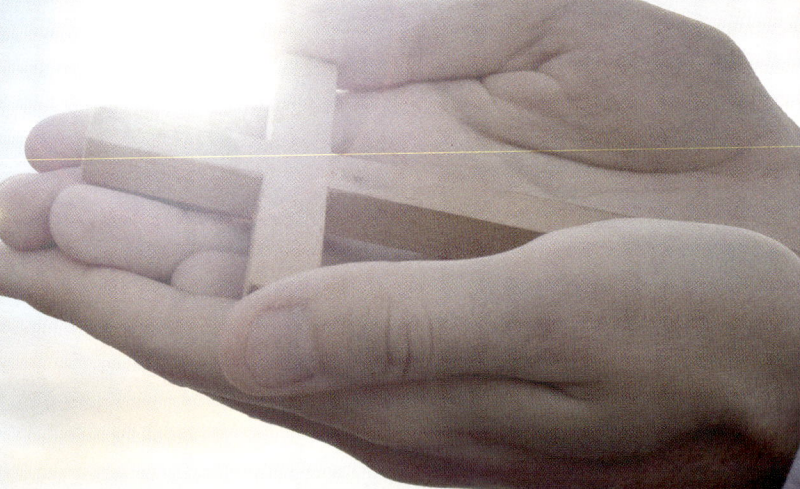